THE
ALL
BETTER
BOOK

THE ALL BETTER BOOK

By Suzy Becker

and hundreds of kids

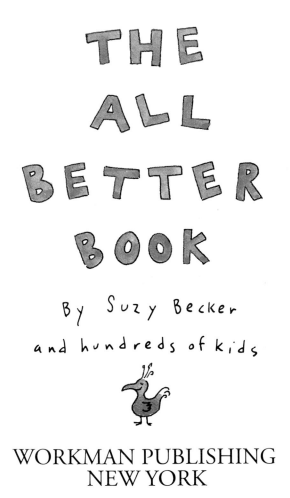

WORKMAN PUBLISHING
NEW YORK

Library of Congress Cataloging-in-Publication Data

Becker, Suzy,
The all better book / by Suzy Becker and hundreds of kids.
p.   cm.
   Summary: Elementary school children present their own ideas about
how to improve the world, by answering such questions as "How would
you go about earthquake-proofing your house?" or "How can men and
women get along better?"
ISBN 1-56305-314-4
1. Children—Quotations.   2. Children—Miscellanea.   [1. Social problems—Miscellanea.   2. Questions and answers.]   I. Title.
PN6084.C5B4   1992
081'.083—dc20   92-50282
                                                          CIP
Workman Publishing   AC
708 Broadway
New York, NY 10003

Manufactured in the United States of America

First printing September 1992

1 3 5 7 9 10 8 6 4 2

For Amy
and my teachers
especially my parents,
Peg Goetze & Lynn Phillips.

SPECIAL THANKS TO:

WORKMAN	WIDGET	AT LARGE
Peter + Carolan		Edite Kroll
Sally Kovalchick	Louise Taylor	
Tom Starace		
Bert Snyder	Deb Van Batenburg	Mary O'Brien
Janet Harris		
David Schiller	Cindy Phillips	
Lisa Eskow		Binky
Nancy Murray	Robbie Kaplan	&
Carbery O'Brien		Wylie
Pat Upton	Sharon Glick	

Key: ▢ PEOPLE   ▢ PETS

"The youth gets together his materials to build a bridge to the moon or perchance a palace or temple on earth, and at length the middle-aged man concludes to build a woodshed with them."
—Henry David Thoreau

Which is why (at the risk of starting my second book with a sentence fragment) I spend most of my Wednesday mornings teaching creative writing to kids.

I know They say with age comes wisdom, but They also say the more you know, the more you know there is to know. And they've really put us in a bind. We have kids growing up thinking adults know the answers, with grown-ups thinking they don't know anything. Being caught right between youth and middle age myself, I began to wonder who was going to solve the world's problems.

One Wednesday, about a year and a half ago, I asked a class of second graders to write down how they'd clean up the oil slicks. Next, I tried having them end all the wars. By the time I got to patching the hole in the ozone, I was pretty sure there wasn't a problem I could pose that kids couldn't solve.

This is a book of *undaunted* wisdom—the result of 80 workshops I held in 20 elementary schools. I like to think it's both a brainstorming challenge for kids and a bridge-building challenge for grown-ups.

To the moon,

Suzy Becker

There is a hole in the ozone, the layer of gas that protects the Earth. How would you repair a hole like that?

Climb up the biggest ladder in the world (which reaches to the moon) and put a giant cork in it.
Katie, age 8

Get some dirt and seeds and plant flowers over the hole to make it look pretty for the aliens.
Sara, age 8

Take a sample of the gas and have scientists make some more and put it back up there.
Joanna, age 7

Make special clothes to protect the Earth in case the hole gets bigger.
Allison, age 8

Use a kaleidoscope to look at the ozone. Then, take super glue, 1,500 band-aids, 28 stickers, one 5 x 9 piece of ice and 5,100 pieces of bubblegum and stick everything on the ozone.
Matthew, age 9

A lot of countries are getting rid of their weapons. But some of the weapons, like tanks, were built so that nothing could destroy them. What should the leaders do with indestructible tanks?

Turn them into animal hospitals.
Amanda, age 8

Turn them into houses for people who don't have houses.
Jennifer, age 7

Make them into museums or offices.
Julia, age 7

Seal up the parts and put them in a playground, so kids could play on them.
Nick, age 8

They put them together, didn't they? They must have the instructions somewhere. Just get the instructions out and do it backwards.
Sylvia, age 8

How can you make people feel better about themselves?

If someone says to me, "I feel that no one likes me," I would say, "Well, I like you and if the people don't like you, they're not the right people for you. But the people that think you're special are special. Because deep inside your heart—<u>way</u> inside—if you really feel deep down, you'll find that you're special."
Reem, age 8

If they don't feel like they're pretty, you could say, "You're a lot prettier than a person I know who has big bulgy eyes."
Katelyn, age 9

Everyone should have an alarm clock that says nice things to them in the morning when they wake up.
Jacqueline, age 8

Everyone is good at something and they should be complimented every day.
Tom, age 8

They should have a call line to cheer people up.
Paul, age 8

As the president of the United States, what would you do personally for all the people without homes?

I would have a building made called the "Free Home Building." And I would have soldiers bring homeless people to it so they will have somewhere to live and someone to talk to.
Charelle, age 9

When people go away, like to their grandparents' house, the homeless people who live near them should live in their houses.
Helena, age 7

I would make friends with a homeless person and let him or her live with me.
Ned, age 8

I would build another Entire State Building just for people without homes.
Kathleen, age 9

I would go door-to-door or tent-to-tent or person-to-person and give food.
Molly, age 8

How about all of the animals without homes?

I love animals, they are so cute. I will take them all home to my house.
Marissa, age 9

Everybody should take one home and make it feel good.
Lamar, age 7

I would build a big place where dogs can live and eat food.
Craig, age 7

Give cats food, a little bath, and no junk food. Let them lick you in the face and don't get angry.
Luis, age 7

There is so much care put into hair, its loss is hard to bear. What do you recommend?

Put a dog or furry animal on his or her head and it will look like hair.
Danny, age 8

Do not live in a city.
Alex, age 8

Make a group to help people without hair.
Harley, age 7

Use Rogaid. If that doesn't work, get a wig. If no wig fits, get a hat. If you don't like to wear hats, glue hair from someone's hairbrush. If everybody you know is bald, put a big bow on your bald spot.
Amanda, age 8

Can you think of a cure for prejudice?

If people act prejudiced, make them wear plaid jackets, plaid shirts, plaid pants and plaid sneakers that say "Don't be prejudiced" on them.
Jonathan, age 10

Everyone should invite someone who is different to their house once a week.
Becca, age 9

Invent a microscopic dot you stick to your clothes that makes you be nice. (Price: $5.00)
Jake, age 9

At the age of 15, 16, 17 or 18 you should go somewhere else in the world for up to five years and make at least one friend.

Josh, age 10

How do you fix someone's broken heart?

Sing a song. Stomp your feet. Read a book.
(Sometimes I think no one loves me so I do one
of these.)
Brian, age 8

Give them some hug bubbles and love them
very much.
Tiffany, age 8

Care for them. Share with them and play
with them.
Shila, age 7

I can take that heart out and put a new heart in.
I would be really sad if my best friend had a
broken heart.
Phu, age 8

What kinds of improvements does our education system really need?

Everyone should have a quiet place to work.
Glorimar, age 9

Make all the floors have thick rugs.
Mariano, age 9

I wish you could learn about math faster.
Lee Ann, age 8

They should let children see their brother or sister at recess.
Jasline, age 8

I would put chocolate milk in the bubbler (water fountain).
Robert, age 8

With billions of people in the world, someone should be able to figure out a system where no one is lonely. What do you suggest?

People should find lonely people and ask them their name and address. Then ask people who aren't lonely their name and address. When you have an even amount of each, assign lonely and not lonely people together in the newspaper.
Kalani, age 8

Make food that talks to you when you eat. For instance, it would say, "How are you doing?" and "What happened to you today?"
Max, age 9

*The government should let all the lonely people pick
a partner and go on vacation with that person.*
Lauren, age 9

We could all visit one lonely person each week.
Shawna, age 9

*We could get people a pet or a husband or a wife
and take them places.*
Matt, age 8

Is there any way to keep kids from joining gangs?

Let them help the police.
Rachel, age 9

Let kids start a radio station with school news on it.
Julia, age 9

Build an underwater dome that kids could play in so they wouldn't get bored.
Greg, age 9

Make a maze race that changes every week.
Colleen, age 8

Have kids make a company that helps people in the neighborhood.
Scott, age 9

What would keep kids away from drugs?

Open a carnival in every town.
Barrett, age 9

Put people together in groups of four and call them the drugbusters and they would have to help each other stay off drugs.
Brendan, age 9

Send kids to stay with people who are famous or to other countries so they can have a good time and forget about drugs.
Marisa, age 9

You would need a special card to get drugs and you could only get it when you are 36.
Carrigan, age 9

There should be a store, and when you are unhappy you could come in and relax or bring a special thing and talk to the person that works there about it.
Tia, age 9

Do you have any advice for people trying to stay young?

My aunt uses Mary Kay.
Sheena, age 7

Have your hair long and healthy.
Amber, age 7

Take a bubblebath every day. And to keep you strong, keep pumping.
Michael, age 8

Keep your imagination or try to lose weight.
Jen, age 8

Get frozen.
Greg, age 7

How would you earthquake-proof your house?

*Put slinkies under it. That
way if it falls down it
will bounce right back up.*
Jonathan, age 8

*Wrap the house in jello so it will
just shake and even if it fell down,
it would still be okay.*
Kelby, age 8

*Put a hot-air balloon on the roof
that would lift your house into
the air when the earthquake came.*
Christie, age 8

Cover the ground with tape so it wouldn't crack.
Geoff, age 8

Glue all your stuff to the floor. If it gets really bad, glue yourself to the floor.
Sara, age 8

What can men and women do to get along better?

My mom should try ice hockey.
   Neil, age 8

*They could understand
better if they listened better.*
Kate, age 8

*Girls like to stay clean and
healthy and brush their
teeth, and boys don't care.*
Chris, age 9

They should just understand that women are more mature than men.
Jennifer, age 8

Men and women shouldn't talk about money.
Julie, age 9

Telling people that smoking is bad for them doesn't always work. What would you do to help them quit?

Call Mother Teresa.
Mary, age 7

*Make a healthy cigarette that doesn't make
people sick.*
Juliana, age 8

*Have a show that makes people laugh so much they
forget about smoking.*
David, age 7

Make cigarettes more expensive.
Rachel, age 7

*Go to a smoker's house and pretend to smoke
and die.*
Alexis, age 8

Do you know of any no-fail diets?

Wear belts every day. (You don't have to do exercises.)
Andrew, age 8

Use exercise shoes—when you get tired and want to go to sleep, too bad! These shoes will make you run until your feet fall off.
Patrick, age 8

Mix Slim-Fast, salt, chopped hot tamales, peanut butter (just a little), eggs, tiny tiny apple slices,

apple sauce, tomato sauce and water. After you eat, go for a jog.
Michael, age 8

Climb the Statue of Liberty and force yourself to eat lima beans.
Hebah, age 7

Help! We're running out of places to put our garbage. What can we do?

Turn the glass into greenhouses.
Michael, age 8

My sister said there's this country with no people.
You can put the garbage in there.
Susan, age 7

Make puppets with old paper bags. And use plastic
bags for tomorrow's lunch.
Stephanie, age 8

Flatten all the cans in a machine and make walls
out of them.
Marlon, age 10

Have a law that every person who litters has to pick
it up and eat it.
Kristin, age 10

It used to be that Russia and the United States were the most powerful countries, at the top of the World Order. Now, because so much has changed so fast, people are saying there will be a new World Order. Who should be at the top?

My parents. Then me, animals, reptiles and my little sister Becky.
Christina, age 7

Kids. The president. Parents. TV. A tree.
Adee, age 7

Kids. Lambs. Me. My mom. Then my teacher.
Molly, age 7

Kids. Chipmunks. Cats, dogs, frogs. Grown-ups. Cheetahs and rabbits.
Matt, age 6

*First snakes. Then me, George Washington, hogs
and my cat.*
Christopher, age 7

People always say "Life's not fair." What's not fair about it?

It's not fair that friends are hard to keep and that they fade away.
Annie, age 8

It's not fair that my brother has a bunk bed.
Christina, age 8

No one should be born with asthma.
Chris, age 7

A chocolate ice cream sundae should be a vegetable so you could eat it with dinner.
Alexander, age 8

It's not fair that my cat gets to go outside and I have to stay in.
Michelle, age 8

Lately, there has been more and more violence in cities. How would you handle a riot?

The whole country should have a big protest together, and all the children should hold up signs that make people stop and laugh and think about what they're doing and how it's disrupting people's lives.
Adrienne, age 9

If it happened in front of my house, I would go outside and tell them that there is no good reason for a war.
April, age 8

I think we should say sorry to the people who get hurt.
Fareeda, age 8

Make blacks equal to whites.
Daris, age 9

What helps people fall asleep when they're afraid?

Saying "when you get up everything will be okay," and piling things up all around them so they feel safe.
Joseph, age 8

Some warm milk and a back rub.
Beth, age 9

Letting the cat sleep with them.
Stephen, age 8

Singing a song to them until they fall asleep.
Elizabeth, age 8

Tell them their guardian angel is there.
Jessica, age 8

When people break the law, we put them in jail. What would you do?

Make them do gymnastics for a month.
Lily, age 7

Make them go to the principal's office and get in very deep trouble.
Ellen, age 7

Have them live with someone who can help them.
Kyle, age 7

Zap them with a ray that doesn't hurt but gets all the bad parts out.
Sam, age 8

I f you would put them in jail,
what should they do?

They should practice being free
and run around while they're
in there.
Alex, age 9

What's the best way to quit biting your nails?

Stick your fingers in dog doo.
Kelly, age 9

Wear shoes on your hands.
Mitchell, age 8

Cut your whole darn nail off and find something better to chew on.
Caitlin, age 9

Put tinfoil on your teeth.
Stephanie, age 9

I bite my nails and my sister does, too. She and I got nail polish stuff that tastes disgusting and it works.
Megan, age 9

What might make it possible to end all the wars?

Give everybody equal things.
Kellie, age 7

Pause all the wars and have the mayors shake hands.
Josh, age 8

Just trade lands. We give them our land and they give us their land.
Wendy, age 7

I would let my uncle stay at home and I would not let people get killed.
Amber, age 8

Do not invent any more war things.
Ryan, age 7

It seems as if people who have things want more things, and then there are even fewer things left for the people who didn't have much to begin with. What should be done?

Parents should not give children whatever they want or they will grow up to be greedy.
Courtney, age 9

Everyone should have to give up one thing.
Matthew, age 9

Try to teach people a lesson by acting like them, and see how they like it.
Katelyn, age 8

I have a friend who is greedy and I told her not to be.
Yajaira, age 10

We should have a contest to see who could share the most.
Robert, age 8

Do you think everything's equal for boys and girls?

Boys should be able to play house or Barbie. Why can't your dad do your hair? I think that for one day girls should be boys and boys can be girls.
Carla, age 8

Boys should be allowed to play with dolls and girls should be allowed to play with waterguns. Men should take turns cooking. Also, men and women should have equal money.
Samantha, age 7

I think girls should be able to play pro baseball, football, hockey and soccer. I also think girls should be able to play boys in tennis.
Jonathan, age 8

I think boys should be able to wear dresses.
Laura, age 8

Too many people spend too many of their waking hours at a job they don't love or even like. Give their bosses some suggestions.

Let people have hamsters on their desks.
Glenda, age 8

Let them make mistakes.
Kerri, age 8

Give a break for five hours.
Yesenia, age 9

Pay double and have a big tickling machine for unhappy workers.
Andrew, age 9

Listen to the workers and respect them and play rock-and-roll music all day.
Holly, age 8

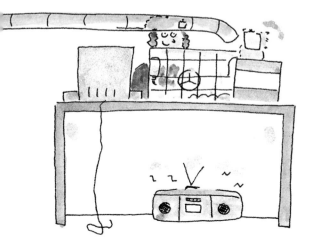

What kinds of things would you do to make life easier for someone who is physically challenged?

I think we should invent rocket packs so people could fly instead of walking.
Justin, age 9

Make a talking cane for people who are blind that would say which way to go.
Matthew, age 9

I would invent a car that drives itself.
Carley, age 9

Maybe when I grow up I will be a doctor.
Kate, age 9

What do you do for good luck?

Pull out an eyelash.
Brendan, age 7

Concentrate, practice and believe in yourself.
Ariele, age 7

Eat cold pizza for breakfast.
Gordon, age 7

Rub a troll's belly.
Holly, age 8

Touch my brother's iguana.
Trista, age 7

Put a penny in my sock.
Alex, age 8

W̲hat would you say to people who say there just isn't enough time in the day?

Eat all your meals at the same time.
Jake, age 8

Read time management books like Manage Your Time Manage Your Work Manage Your Life.
Ben, age 9

Don't get lost.
Brad, age 8

Put another number on your clock.
Lynn, age 8

Only watch the news once a day.
Myles, age 9

It seems as if the longer we live, the shorter our memories get. What can we do about this?

Eat broccoli.
William, age 8

Tell a parakeet everything and bring it with you everywhere.
Jacqueline, age 7

Make a picture in your mind of what you are trying to remember.
Christina, age 9

Write stuff on your pants.
Jose, age 8

How can we take better care of our water?

Put suntan lotion on all the animals. Then take the water out and wash it in a washing machine and put it back.
Kathryn, age 8

Have scientists make fish that love to eat tons of pollution.
Jackie, age 9

Put a raccoon in the water with a bathing suit on to gather up all the garbage.
Kim, age 8

Get a big sponge and tie it with ropes to a helicopter. Then lower it down and soak up all the oil.
Meghan, age 8

God would take all the water and the angels would clean it drop by drop. Then God would make it rain and everything would fill up again.
Matt, age 9

What would you do about the smog that hangs over big cities?

Call the newspaper and tell them to write: Don't drive so much! Walk more!
Jena, age 7

I'd stop what makes smog for a day.
Donna, age 7

*I would have all the people get a hose
and wash the smog away every day.
It might make a rainbow.*
Johanna, age 8

*I would drop a vacuum cleaner from a plane
with a parachute and turn it on. (Make sure that
the wires are very very long.)*
Amy, age 7

Parents are full of suggestions for kids. How about giving them a few of your own?

I wish that my mom would take me out by myself. And if I want to make a cake, she will help me.
Rosemary, age 8

I wish they would let me play outside 19 hours a day, and they could let me have ten wolves in my room. They could also make my favorite dinner every day and pay me one dollar for housecleaning.
Carlos, age 9

I wish my mom would let me go to her job with her.
Theresa, age 9

The only thing I would change about my mom is her camera. She is always taking pictures of the new baby.
Ivonne, age 8

I wish they would take me to Burger King every day so I could win the hidden surprise and then I could go to Disney World.
Dagoberto, age 9

People usually tell the truth, but sometimes they don't. How could you know for sure when to believe them?

They should make a spray that would make someone's clothes change color or their hair turn gray or their ears stick out when they lied.
Megan, age 8

I always know when people are lying. They smile or get nervous and crush their hands, or they don't look up or they laugh.
Nancy, age 9

When people lie, their faces look wrong.
Fred, age 8

You can always tell when it's something you know, like when someone says my three-year-old puppy can jump over a fence. You know that's a lie.
Jennifer, age 9

If people always had their moms there, they would be scared to lie.
Margie, age 9

The government is sort of broke. How can it raise money?

The president should get a job.
Brian, age 9

The president could sell icies or play Bingo.
Betsy, age 8

The government could have a bake sale.
Jennifer, age 9

Have them: I. *Try a lemonade stand.* 2. *Write a book.* 3. *Work at McDonald's or Burger King.* 4. *Be a teacher.*
Pamela, age 8

They should have a garage sale of all the stuff they don't need.
Jonathan, age 8

How would you take care of someone who's sick and isn't going to get better?

I would let them have their pet in bed with them.
And I would make medicine that tastes good.
Noelle, age 8

I think everybody who is sick like that should be able to have pancakes every morning and a trip somewhere and not have to worry about chores.
Robbie, age 7

I would stay by their side.
Marina, age 8

I would treat them like they're rich.
Steven, age 8

> *I would let them lie down in bed and try to whisper so they don't have a headache.*
> Ashley, age 8

Some people are always shy, and everybody is shy sometimes. How can you help a shy person feel braver?

Hold their hand.
Christine, age 7

Sometimes you're not shy, you're just quiet.
Tiffany, age 7

*Make jokes like, "Knock, knock! Who's there? Pizza.
Pizza who? Pizza! Give me pepperoni."*
Denise, age 8

Ask them to sit with you.
Elisa, age 8

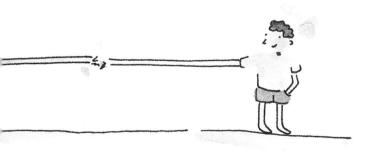

Grown-ups need to have more fun. What do you suggest?

Run through the sprinkler.
Kate, age 8

Celebrate their birthday every day.
Jennifer, age 8

Have more boyfriends.
Jessica, age 7

We should read to them and play with them more.
Michael, age 8

Watch Oprah Windfield.
Michaela, age 7

How can you show that you love your country?

Help sick people.
Emily, age 8

Be a selectman.
Paul, age 9

Use both sides of your paper.
Christina, age 7

Have a big flag hanging on your house.
Patrick, age 9

Always carry a credit card.
Emily, age 8

People start to think all the news is bad news. Let's hear some good news for a change.

I got a new bike. And I'm having macaroni tonight.
Caitlin, age 8

I made a new friend.
Brian, age 8

When you look in your desk and you find the teacher's edition.
Jeffrey, age 8

My two aunties are each having a baby.
Lynne, age 8

People are eating more fruit.
James, age 8

The biggest challenge of all might be getting people up off their couches to go out and make the world better. Any ideas?

Put spikes on all the couches.
Micah, age 10

Run a commercial that says, "If you do not turn off your TV, we will cancel all TV shows."
Ben, age 9

You should have to clean up for a year every 10 years that you live.
Emily, age 10

Have a huge speaker that puts people in a trance to fix the world.
Bash, age 10

Start doing something yourself, or get someone who a lot of people like to start something.
Julia, age 10

"*To laugh often and much, to win the respect of intelligent people and the respect of children; to earn the appreciation of honest critics and endure the betrayal of false friends; to appreciate beauty, to find the best in others, to give of oneself; to leave the world a bit better, whether by a healthy child, a garden patch or a redeemed social condition, to have played and laughed with enthusiasm and sung with exultation; to know even one life has breathed easier: this is to have succeeded.*"

—Ralph Waldo Emerson

I'd like to thank the following Teachers, Principals and their Student-Authors for their help with this book:

Sue Abrams
Luanne Allard
Pat Aubuchon
Walter Bell
Judy Blatt
Bob Blue
Mary Lou Brodeur
Donna Camponizzi
Gloria Cartagena
Ruth Cohen
Adrienne Daly
Holley Daschbach
Leslie DePaolo
Karen Devlin
Kathleen DiBenedetto
Janice Donahue
Myrna Estes
Susan Fontaine
Cecilia Franzel
Sheila Gedney
Sae Ghose
Grace Gielich
Kate Greaney

Karen Grubb *(my third-grade teacher)*
Ann Guilfoile
Meynardo Gutierrez
Joanne Hamilton
Peg Humphrey
Erin Keaney
Marilyn Kipp
Mary Ann Longwell
Anne Larrow
Marge Lee
Melissa Lee
Ruth Levey
Suzanne Logan
Karen Lowe
Helen McElroy
Marilyn McGinn
Wendy Marotta
Elaine Marzilli
Mary Beth Melican
Mary Ann Moll
John Monfredo
Lynn Morrissey
Jane Moynihan
Alberta Natoli

Barbara Noun
Eric Pell
Margery Pell
Lisa Perlman
Sandy Phillips
Joan Pirrello
Dawn Quinlan
Priscilla Rhodes
Susan Riley
Mary Ripley
Peggy Roberts
Amy Robinson
Carol Robinson
Helen Robinson
Penny Scarano
Susan Schroeder
Jean Shannon
Carol Shilinsky
Kerry Siano
Mena Topjian
Patricia Tucker
Eileen Vogel
Jeanne Watson
Andrea Purcell Wong